The Love Kit

Katharine Angelina Love

AOS Publishing, 2025

Copyright © 2025

Katharine Angelina Love

ISBN: 978-1-998662-40-1

Cover Design: Chanelle Poupart

Visit AOS Publishing's website:
www.aospublishing.com

for you

the rainiest day

rain rain cold rain
making my heart hurt
making my bones ache
making my tears freeze
as they trickle down
my face on this dreary
damp friday morning.

i'm taking a shortcut
through the partially
frozen field my running
shoes already soaked
through, returning the
milk that has soured
before it's stamped
expiry date.

i'm feeling just like that
bottle of milk curdled
before my time.

the rain is coming
down harder and
harder now i wish
so badly that i
still had my car
so that i could drive
to the store but my
car has disappeared
with my lover alongside
all hopes of safety
and permanence.

the storm is reaching
its apex raining like
cats and dogs ~

where does that idiom
'raining cats and dogs'
come from anyway?

i really wish it was
actually raining cats
and dogs this very
moment for i would
scoop up a little
bedraggled puppy
and place her
underneath my yellow
slicker next to my heart,
where she could
snuggle up close to my
body, her body
understanding
that finally against all
odds,
she has been saved
from the cold.

mix tape

if i was blessed
enough to
have a lover;
i would imagine
us together in
our queen size bed
with the wrought iron
headboard ~
her, the big spoon
me the small,
lying so close
together, allowing
the early morning
sun to warm our
achy old bones.

she might ask me
then, as we were lying
all comfy and cozy
if there was anything
special i wanted
for my upcoming
birthday, and i
might say
"yes, my sweetness,
i would love for
you to make me
a mix tape."

this tape would
be concrete
proof, a test of her
love and devotion.

i know, i know,
there should be no

test to prove one's
love, but for me,
being known,
being seen, and
being witnessed,
feels so much
like being loved
for if she does
loves me, if
she truly truly
wants to pledge
her troth to mine,
she will know
instinctively
which music to
choose to make
me understand
that I am not
alone in this
world, anymore.

i remember

i remember one sunny
august day in jackson's point,
the tar so wonderfully warm on
my very flat feet.
i remember being so excited
to buy my first record album
'the bay city rollers',
placing it gently down on my
dad's old record player with the
worn alligator handle.

i remember gently tracing the
three brown freckles on debbie
dankoff's nose.

i remember walking home one
day from second grade, thinking
recess was actually lunchtime
and how shamed i felt at my faux
pas.

i remember the smell of jane's
favourite plaid shirt: a heady
combination of tobacco and juicy
fruit gum.

i remember eating my bubbie's
white fish, potatoes and carrots
out of my very favourite but
now slightly flawed beatrix potter
bowl, the chip obscuring the
bunny's right ear.

i remember floating on a red
and blue striped raft in st.tropez
totally zenned out by the soft

motion of the sea.

i remember pulling the ace of
pentacles from my worn deck of
tarot cards and winning one
hundred dollars from a bingo
scratch card later that very same
day.

i remember hiking up mt.
mansfield with my circus puppy
georgia gray, my right toe chafing
at the tip of my worn out
blundstone's thinking; yes it
hurts, but soon we will be there.

missing u

i miss the u
that was part of us.
i miss saying
"i'll have to ask my
girlfriend"
before committing us
to any social engagements.

i miss the late
night after date
night kisses.

i miss waking up
in the early
hours of the morning
from a bad dream
to find your hand
placed ever so
gently on the small
of my back.

i miss your raucous
laugh that made
people glare as you
laughed even harder
and said "let them stare
baby, let them stare."

i miss slowly licking
the juice off
your fingers from
the plums that we
shared together
on the kitchen floor
after making love
all night long.

i miss calling you
from the train to
let you know that
i'll be home at
eleven and not nine,
because the train
broke down in the
middle of nowhere,
but we are all safe
and i can't wait
until you can hold me
in your arms again.

i miss the u
that was part of us.

and dream of you

soft flannel sheets,
the sharp green
scent of tea.
slow cello music,
your body holding
my body.

every night in my
dreams you come
to me..
but only
in my dreams,
because you
are a we
and your we
didn't ever
include me.

i shouldn't have
been surprised
at this turn of events,
you were a
we long before you
ever met me.

you told me that
you'd been waiting
for me for eons,
for lifetimes,
for forever
and though you
shouldn't, you must
have me and
even if i
wanted to say no,
even if i could

have said no,
i said yes,
i wanted you, too.

so we began and
here we are
four years in,
all your earnest
trust me's having
collapsed like
waves into the sea,
into the sea
that you love
so much, into your
vastness that holds
everything but me.

yet i stay here
like cinderella,
slipper in hand
waiting for you
to claim me
like lost baggage,
holding my breath
for days at a time
because breathing
requires me
to be here,
but all i want to do
is lie down
on my couch,
and dream of
soft flannel sheets,
the sharp green
scent of tea,
slow cello music
and your body,
holding my body.

lifeboat

feel your rage
feel your grief
feel your joy
feel everything-
don't outsource
your feelings
don't send out
your little wounded
child alone to
find her safe harbour.

hold on to her as
if she's the last
passenger on the
titanic and you
her only lifeboat.

trust your own heart,
let go of everything -
all the detritus
all the clutter
that has busied
your heart for
the past one
thousand lifetimes.

you are safe now,
you are held now,
welcome home.

atonement

many decades ago
i made a pilgrimage
to the wailing wall
along with hundreds
of other supplicants,
here to place ever
so reverentially
their wishes into
those ancient cracks.

given the opportunity
to face again
those broken stones,
this time around
i would leave my
magical thinking behind,
because no prayer
i could fashion
would have made me
look like joni mitchell
despite my desperate
pleas to the god
of my ancestors.

today, i would
offer up instead
this simple prayer
for myself and for
sentient beings
everywhere:

a prayer of surrender ~
may i stop resisting
what is and allow
the healing
to enter my body,

letting every fiber
of my being know
that i am loved by
something bigger
than my broken.

relaxing into the
revelation that i
am exactly enough.
no edits,
no modifications
needed to
love my body
for my body
(and your body, and all bodies)
have always been
a wonderland.

menemsha

darling:
long have i waited breath
by breath for your arrival.
i must be honest here my love,
there were times
days//months//years
when i thought
you would never appear,
yet here you are;
bones and pulse
and skin,
no longer a figment,
a fragment,
a fervent wish.

the totality of your love
forces me to acknowledge
slowly, ever so slowly,
that i am deserving of
kindness and a place in this
world.

i love getting lost in
the deep of you, feeling
joined in a way i've
never felt before,
my own unified
theory.

memories of menemsha,
the winter of our content,
searching for sea glass
on the frozen beach,
your sturdy arms
protecting me from
the harsh wind that

blew sand into our
eyes and mouths,
and hair.

i remember how we ran
together into a cove,
seeking shelter
from a sudden snowstorm.

i kissed the nape
of your neck, your skin
oh your skin, tasting
so sweet; a heady
mixture of pure maple
syrup, along with your own
dusky pheromones,
making your scent
so potent, i could
find you in the dark.

despite the dampness
of the wet sand,
i felt a sense of warmth
infuse my body,
a knowing that
you will be here,
a heart without
question,
someone to watch over
me.

even now

3 a.m.
can't sleep turning
my pillow over
and over
to find
the cool side

ruminating over lost
opportunities and
roads not taken.

mary oliver
once wrote
that you do not
have to be good ~
but if i am
not good
then who am i?

is my unadorned
(more than)
slightly tarnished self
still worthy of love?

all those thoughts
trickle through my
mind as i stare
up at the ceiling,

praying to the stain
in the grain
of the wood
that looks like jesus.

torch song for the little bird

early morning light
softly illuminates
the etching of a
bird on my blush
coloured wall.

"be careful with whom
you share your little
efforts at staying
luminescent."

says the brown bird,
perhaps a wren,
perhaps a swallow.

"now is the
time to bring
your brightest self
to the world,
even though."

i said to my small
unfurling self that
is almost ready
to fly.

she is my drug

she is my drug,
my medicine, my
poison.
i wait helplessly,
hopelessly praying
for the text that
doesn't come,
for the phone
that doesn't ring,
for her lips to land oh so
gently on my mouth.

i grasp her tibetan crystal
that she bought me
last october in my
left hand, praying
to every single buddhist
deity, begging them
for help for us to
reconnect somehow
through the ethers,
through the eons,
through to this
moment —
so i won't have
to feel this aching
aloneness, this thump, thump,
thump of terror -
that my mother was right,
i am unlovably broken and
wrong.

my arrhythmic heart
waits for that very
slim, silver sliver of a
moment when she calls

and i am quieted
like a weighted blanket
dropped around my soul
then just as quickly,
she leaves and i'm
thrust back into my indigo
midnight where no-thing
ever appears, only
no-thing is actually
some thing, that whispers
my name and tells me
i will be alone and
without safety, for the
rest of my days.

charms

i collect mothers
like charms on a
bracelet, heavy on my wrist;
always on the hunt
for just one - more.

my covert obsession,
always scanning the
sidewalk for another,
more luminous than the
last, longing for that
glimpse of my past
that never was and
never could be.

i felt her before
i saw her, passing
me on the street
last tuesday, kind eyes
shimmering, light -
filled, imbued with grace.

i brushed up
against her body
almost casually, just
to share a few words,
to experience the soft
touch of her hand
on my shoulder
as I breathed her warmth
into my frozen core.

"i'm so sorry" i say..
(i will lie prostrate
in the gutter for you)
"it's all right my dear"

she says,
(she has no subtext).

i fall into her subtle
embrace silently hoping
maybe this time,
just for this moment,
i could believe
she was mine.

my real life mother
is the antithesis of soft,
all hard lines and
planes, no give there ..
no breathing space
for me to arrive.

this morning, lying
in my bed watching
the light show display
from my heart - shaped
mobile, a thought
kept trilling though
my mind like a
tiny hopeful birdie..
what if .. what if ..
i can raise myself
out of my mother stupor
and the fugue state
i find myself in whenever
we are together.

if i can do this one
very hard thing, then i
might be able to
leave my bracelet
behind, tucking it safely
into my indigo velvet
pouch that carries the
ashes of my beloved pup

gucci love and
hold myself afloat
by a red string
of hope, a belief
that i can indeed
someday become
the woman i have
always hungered for.

the birdcage

tell me dear one, is today the
day you decide to break free?
no breaking necessary of course,
you have possession of the keys.
perhaps you've forgotten that
you hid them in a secret
compartment deep in the bottom
of your cage,
underneath all the bird droppings
and old newspapers.

i get it, you feel safe in there.
you share your cage with a
turquoise cockatoo you've
named eleanor blue.
eleanor saves her favourite
crackers for you, in return you've
taught her to swear.
you find it strangely comforting
when she screams
"gabh suas ort fein!" in
gaelic at the television screen
while a reporter shares another
calatimous news story.

i understand, i have safety
issues of my own.
i'm afraid of sudden loud noises
and black widow spiders.
i wake up most nights shaking
after another apocalyptic
end of the world nightmare.

why should you then, my friend
want to leave your comfy cozy
cage?

i shall tell you why –
because i've discovered that
despite everything,
beauty infuses every centimetre
of our world.
beauty is out there for you to
claim like a prize, like a
benediction sent as a directive
from the universe to you.

can you choose faith over
complacency?
come fly with me.
together we will
open ourselves up
to the world,
breath by breath,
bird by bird.

this is the place where i rest

learning how to stop
blowing up my life
from the inside out
has been a challenge
for me beginning with
my arrival, no
body there to soften
my fall so i fell hard
into days and nights
of non - stop stuffing
my face with food,
always looking for comfort
always looking for faster
and faster ways to
stop feeling so much pain.

i knew that marrying
him was a sin against
myself but i, so
desperate for a tribe
of little me's
and my family's praise,
failed to hear my
timorous voice that said
"no, no, no."

today, after decades of
abasement, i claim
myself.
finally, finally i choose
myself over the pain,
over the food, over
the disassociation,
over the chaos.

i am now ready

to commit myself
to this one
wild and precious life.

ocean

your ocean is
calling my name –
enticing me with
your siren song.

your eyes –
two separate bodies
of water, bluegreen
waves of light.

when you kiss
my clit i feel
anointed by the
deep crimson velvet
thrust of your tongue,
warm holding salty wet.

glimpses of other lifetimes
dancing unfettered
naked under
our indigo sky.

baubles and bling

he slipped into the booth
adjacent to mine this
morning at the
coffee shop down
the street from
my studio apartment.

he told me his name
was hugh, when i asked
if louie and dewey
were coming to
join him, he did not
appear to be
amused. perhaps he
was averse to ducks,
or more likely, me.

hugh was lit from
the inside - he seemed
both birthday candles
and birthday cake.

my heartbeat.
my hunger.
i want it,
i want it.

hugh was wearing
a large beaded tiger's
eye bracelet on his
left wrist that immediately
grabbed my attention.

i had to have one
just like his, even
though i had long

ago given up on
jewelry, even though
i had long ago
given up on men.

my heartbeat.
my hunger.
i want it,
i want it.

i lusted after his
bracelet knowing if
i owned one just
like hugh's, his super
powers would flow
from his bracelet
directly to me.

hugh told me about
jasmine who sold
her jewelry from
her home across
from his yoga studio.

of course he practiced
yoga, i'm certain he
brought his own
mat made out of
organically grown hemp.

after some gentle prodding,
hugh gave me jasmine's
number. i could feel
myself inching closer
to the magic.

my heartbeat.
my hunger.
i want it,
i want it.

i sent jasmine a text
and she responded
instantly.
"come right away"
she said. "i live in st. henri."

this meant nothing to me
since i am directionally
challenged on the
best of days.

"is that far?" i asked.
"i don't have a car, and i'll
be walking with my dog
georgia gray."

"it's not far at all" said jasmine.
"just walk all the way
down greene street,
then take a left onto
saint jacques."

so off we go,
my puppy georgia gray
and me, intrepid
journeywoman and
her trusted canine
companion.

except that it doesn't
take us twenty minutes,
or thirty minutes
or even forty, but
i tell myself i don't
care because it's all
downhill, because it's
a sunny day,
because georgia gray
is happy, because

the eye of the tiger
is calling me home.

i reach my destination
and knock boldly on
her crimson coloured
door.

a full bodied woman
wearing a vintage
japanese kimono greets
us and says
"welcome, i'm jasmine!"

my heartbeat.
my hunger.
i want it,
i want it.

i said "jasmine, i have
been walking on
my hands and knees
for a hundred miles
through the city
repenting."

"well then" said she.
"you must be very thirsty!"

she offered georgia gray
and me water from her well.
i had never tasted
water so pure and so
sweet.

jasmine brought out
her baubles
for me to admire.
she had bracelets made
of amethysts and garnet

lapis and hematite.

she had bracelets
made of silver and gold,
copper and pewter, but
no tiger's eye in sight.

i asked jasmine
if she could make
me the same bracelet
that she made for hugh.

"i'm so sorry" said jasmine
"hugh is divine incarnate.
i made that bracelet
exclusively for him."

and just like that,
with one little snap,
i was banished from the
island where hope and hearth
and family reside and i most
definitely, now never will.

my heartbeat.
my hunger.
i *want it.*
i want it.

i couldn't help myself,
my eyes immediately
filled with tears.

jasmine offered up a
consolation prize,
a bracelet made of
hawk's eye. hawk's eye?
i don't think so!

i was not a graceful

loser, always mortified
to come in second.

so there i was,
my tears staining
her cherry wood table,
as jasmine gently
took my hand and
placed the bracelet
on my wrist.

"look katharine," she said.
"tiger's eye represents
the sun, but hawk's eye
represents the moon,
and didn't you just
tell me that gray is
your favourite colour?"

i did and it is
plus i keep a portrait
of artemis,
goddess of the hunt
and the moon on
 my night table
beside my bed.

i know my hunger -
my wanting,
will never be sated
by donuts and
dim sum,
baubles and bling,
winning medals of honour
or donning angel wings.

i get that, i truly do.
but the wanting,
my wanting, is the
closest i've gotten

to feeling tethered
to something tangible,

so for a moment,
for that one
brief wanting moment,
i can stop feeling
that i'm here, dangling all
alone on the edge
of the earth.

my heartbeat.
my hunger.
i want it.
i want it.

6 a.m. christmas morning

6 a.m. christmas morning
i awake, shivering.

i turn on my heating
pad and pretend
that this is you, warming
up my cold,
keeping me protected
from the frigid air
that has found its way
through my broken
balcony door.

i wrap my arms tightly
around my body
imagining that my hands
were your hands,
by some christmas miracle
of transmutation.

you my darling,
are my home,
my haven, my safe
space where i
come for sanctuary,
for solace whenever
this world of mine gets
too overwhelmingly real.

someday soon i
shall feel your
tender arms around me;
in the meantime i carry
your warmth with
me like those little
hand warmers that

activate when you
break them apart.

you are and will
always be the
match to my flame.

much

"i'm too
much"
she said.

"too much
need, too much
neurosis, too much
muchness"

"i don't think
you are too
much" i said

"i think you are
amazing!"

"really?" she said
as the tears fell,
"because i so don't
feel amazing."

"in fact i
feel the opposite
of amazing,
dull and small
and inconsequential."

"i know I'm too much,"
she continued.
"i was told at least
ten thousand times
the record stuck
on repeat,
so much that
the words
too much

are tattooed on
my bones
and my ligaments
and my heart."

i told her that
yesterday i
saw a tiny dimpled
and dented copper
thimble sitting on
a faded penny
in an antique store
and thought,
"this is what
she thinks
she deserves,
a thimble
just a thimble
of love
sitting on a coin
that is out
of circulation"

but that's so
not true, she
deserves all the
stars in the night sky.
she deserves every
beautiful seashell and
well worn glass
from every sea,
she deserves me.

love in the time of covid

she said " i have ten minutes
can we talk?"
yes of course we can talk,
i was just writing the
last stanza in my poem
that i had been working on
for hours, but i would
drop almost everything
to have a moment with her,
no matter how brief, just
to be given the chance
to hear her voice, slightly
torqued due to the tinny sound
quality of my iphone speaker.

my back is beginning
to feel stiff as i wait for
her call in my rickety
wicker chair, but i
don't move for fear
of breaking our tenuous
but profound essence
to essence connection.

could i finally be
falling in love?
i feel so exposed
and vulnerable
here, everything feels
much more complicated
during these pandemic times.

we made a plan to meet
halfway between her home
and mine but then covid
put the kibosh on our

rendezvous by closing the
border, now no one knows when
they might reopen and then
there's the problem of her
partner...

i have always prided myself
on my colour inside the lines
ethical code and clearly
designated boundaries,
however it seems at
this moment in time i am
currently ethically free.

i tell myself all that matters
is when we speak
i stop holding my breath,
and begin to sync my
breath with her breath,
and then we breathe
together as one.

finally after decades
of holding myself together so
tightly, i feel myself unraveling
into her energetic embrace.

the uncertainty of it all is
playing havoc with my heart,
as i wait in my rickety
wicker chair, leaning
in to the hum of the moment.

in the absence of hope

in the absence of hope
nothing grows:
fires succumb,
stars lose their twinkle
and yet there is a
certain relief
--- release ---
from the fairytale that
was told to you
from the beginning;
that love conquers hate
(or apathy), that good
vanquishes evil,
that a kiss from
the queen shall
wake you from
your seasonal slumber.

so much effort
invested in resisting
what is here in this
place called the present.

if you can stop for
one second
(or possibly two)
you would see that
the opposite of resisting
is allowing;
allowing for the
sputtering of hope,
allowing for the
finality of death -
of the dream,
of the fantasy,
into something deeper

and more profound
(than your ever imagined
mind can imagine)
relaxing into the
inevitable now.

reverb

i felt you before
i saw you..
soft breeze, diffused light,
a stirring, a rustling,
the homecoming
of a rare and
delicate creature.

my world shifted,
a portal opened
into the room
with a view
that i believed
had been closed off
to me forever
when my eyes
first met yours.

forgiveness

knowing when
to stop eating
smoking, loving,
obsessing, has
always been
difficult for me,
starting at the
beginning when there
was no soft place
to fall, so i fell into food
and cigarettes and boys
and then girls, always
looking for comfort,
always looking for ways
to make the pain
stop coming faster
and faster like a train
with faulty brakes~
never stopping my
obsessive thoughts
of belonging to a small
tribe of *me's*.
walking down the aisle
asking god to forgive me,
knowing that marrying
was a sin against
myself, but my family
happy i was now normal,
and i, so desirous
of welcome, ignoring my
small whispering voice that said
"no. no. no."

this time around i
shall open my heart
to the kindness

that surrounds me,
saying yes to myself
saying no to
the unhealthy,
forgiving myself
over and over
and over again.

the promise

can i, could i let myself go?
what does letting go even look like?
shorn hair, makeup free face,
running shoes instead of heels.
comfort over style.
what does it mean to let oneself
go?
and where would i be going?
perhaps home to myself, where i
can embrace the all of me.
born with moebius syndrome*
my eyes, my mouth, were
differently put together, one might
even say *queerly* made.
i love that word queer,
the hard q,
and those long e's..
so here i am, on a cloudless
wednesday morning,
remembering the promise
i had made to myself all those
years ago..
that no matter what,
i would never abandon myself.
and i have, for years, for
decades, for eons.

but now, after
too many false starts and stops,
i've finally come home.
*moebius syndrome is a rare congenital condition which causes
facial paralysis and limited eye movement, often accompanied
by hearing loss, autism spectrum disorder, limb differences,
chronic fatigue, speech and dental concerns.

a poem for the weary

3:30 a.m. scrolling
through tiktok like a baby
with her binky.
i watch a bulldog
with a bandana
skateboarding,
and a young man
with an asmr voice
talks to me about
buying a birkin bag.

i'm so lonely.
i haven't been touched
in such a long time that
i can't even remember the
feeling of being held.

i just feel this need,
this pull, like someone
who has lost a limb
feels this phantom tingling,
a yearning for something
that once was there and
is now irretrievably gone.

what love is:
a poem in three parts

part one:
it's 2:30 in the morning
and once again i'm
in the bathtub trying to
relax, trying to heat myself
up so that i may fall
back to sleep,
when i realize suddenly
how thirsty i am.

i just can't bring myself
to leave my now
perfectly warmed rose
scented bath.

part two:
this is the moment
where i wish i had
a partner to whom
i could whisper softly
through the open door
so as not to disturb
our neighbours..
"darling, can you please
bring me a glass of
ice water along with those
juicy ripe figs that we
picked up earlier this
evening from the
st. lawrence market?

part three:

love is a verb.
love is not kissing

your wife's picture
whilst extolling her
virtues.
love is getting out of
your comfy cozy bed
at 2:30 in the morning
because you hear love's
voice in the guise of
your wife, breaking
through your slumber,
imploring you to please
bring a tall icy glass
of water with some
figs to the bathroom for
your beloved.

what is a love poem?

what is a love poem?
just some words
strung together -
my heart, her hands, our lips.
we met by happenstance,
we met by divine intervention,
we met by the seashore.

i fell instantaneously in love.
i fell into her embrace.
i fell.
we've waited months
for this day.
we've waited hours
for this moment.
we've waited lifetimes.

i was terrified.
i was flummoxed.
i was in love.

her body invited
me in.
her eyes told me
she was safe.
her mouth gave
me everything.

three days were
all we had.
three days of sanctuary,
three days to
dissolve the illusion that
we were ever apart.

four thousand three hundred

and twenty minutes,
feels like eons,
feels like
seconds..
though more is
often thought better,
sometimes less is truly
more.

she brought solace
to my soul..
this is a love poem.

begging for crumbs

i've been so hungry
 for love.
i've been so hungry
for some thing but
there is no thing
here so I devour
an entire chocolate cake
and my fork
and my knife,
and even my spoon.

all through my tumultuous
childhood i kept
tumbling down
the barren hole of
my loneliness,
so deep the crevasse,
so desperate was i
for affection or just
a gentle hand
to hold my little hand.

i tried and tried to grab
hold of anything
to stop my downward
spiral, a snow petrel,
an icy ledge, but the enormity
of my need kept
propelling me down
and down and down
the icy darkness.

i tried begging
to be heard
then shouting
to be heard

then screaming
to be heard
trying so hard
to find someone
to help me out
of my cold hell of a hole,
howling for so long
that my voice had become
ragged with pain,
hoarse from the grief
of it all.

my earliest memories -
waking up in a
hospital crib, sheets all
bloodied and no one
there to offer a
reason nor to offer solace.

i was only three years old
when i got lost
in a shopping mall
because my parent
could not parent and
somehow forgot
i was supposed
to be there,
by her side.

books were so
much safer than family
so i got lost inside
books along with
two dozen oreo cookies
and a tall glass of
milk, sweets to
ameliorate my bitterness
of living with family
who seemingly hurt me
just for sport.

what do you do when
you just don't count
to anyone?

you count yourself out ..
out of school, out of work,
out of love, out of life.

i was so desperate
to taste that beautiful
buttered piece of
raisin bread at my family's
breakfast table that
i tried to grab the first
fresh slice, but
my hands were
too slow, all the bread
was already gone,
the only thing left for me
were the crumbs.

decades came and
decades went.
life happened around me
but never through me.

then one day, which
happened to be my birthday,
i woke up and i
told myself that today
i would begin my day
by choosing myself.

that today i would begin
my day by being
kind to myself.
that today i would
begin my day by
loving myself.

and i baked
(all by myself!)
the most beautiful
birthday cake
and blew out all my candles,
celebrating my own happy
beginnings.

finally, finally i could
begin to feast
on my own life.

languishing

i languish in the language
of the victim.
until i let go of
this particularly
painful pleasure,
i shall stay stuck
in the muck of
my own making,
force feeding
my feral ferocious
voice into the
deepest crevice of
my core, my
passport stamped
with repeat visits
to heartbreak hotel.

but not in this moment -
in this moment i snap
the rose quartz bracelet
i have placed on my
right wrist, stopping for a
nanosecond my spiraling,
so that i may rest
in the stillness and
the beauty of my
perfectly flawed
self.

rainbow soap

i still keep a small piece
of rainbow soap that
she gave me on our
last vacation together,
left high up on a metal
corrugated shelf
in my shower stall.

a tiny multi coloured
remnant of all the
moments that we've
shared.

i moved it yesterday
to the highest shelf
for protection, once
i realized that it was
slowly disappearing and
that unless something
miraculous happens
(and it might, though the
older i get, the less i believe
in divine intervention),
she too shall slowly
dissolve into the ethers ..

there's a minuscule part
of me however, that
still believes she will
come back to me, for
how could she not?
how would it be
possible for one to
leave such a
profound love?

apparently it was scorch
the earth difficult for her
but she did ultimately
chose to dissolve our
once tightly tethered
red cord of connection.

it wasn't only our love story
that ended, but the death
of my dream of being
saved, of being saved
by love, saved from a
lifetime of loneliness
and reservations
for one.

and so here i am,
once again, back
in my shower, baptized
by the water, born again
into this unwieldy wild,
yet ultimately beautiful
life where i belong,
where i finally, finally
belong to the holy
trinity of me, myself and i.

the glorious middle

what are we all
searching so
desperately for?

a touch, a smile,
a fleeting thrill of
acknowledgment
that belies this truth -
that we are alone
here in the beginning
and we are alone
here in the end.

but my friends,
in the glorious middle..
that's when we rise up
with all that we have
to cleave together
making the knowledge
of our inevitable end
more opaque,
more distant,
more manageable.

death shall never
find us here in this
so much happiness
space where
love protects our
most vulnerable
edges and our still
beating hearts.

phoenix

can't she see
she's ruined me?
but she can't see,
she never could
and now
i almost know,
she never will.

but did she ruin me?
i'm still here.
i've survived all of
my worst days despite
her best efforts to
annihilate.

i rise, phoenix style,
the earth scorched
from the ashes
of my despair.

i'm standing here
on holy ground,
anointed by the
salted water of
my tears.

i am deserving
of a second chance
to fly fast and high,
those burnt orange
feathers, bright and
gleaming in my dawn's
early light.

begin again

walk
talk
swirl
twirl
laugh
cry
decide
deny
hug
shrug
indulge
divulge
masturbate
collaborate
spoon
swoon
kiss
miss
envelop
develop
dance
prance
reach
teach
illuminate
ruminate
elevate
celebrate
inhale
exhale
live
love
weep
reap
sleep

begin again

worthy

i was born without
a left cheekbone
my tongue just a
nub of pink.

failure to thrive
pronounced the doctor
and so my mother
believing the male doctor god,
decided this shall be
my life sentence
condemning me to listen
forever to her
hypnotic tune of toxic
shame and blame.

after my first few months
on the planet,
all the appropriate
bones and muscles
grew in except for
a tiny muscle
in my tongue
which led to a very
small but perceptible
speech impediment.

leaving me feeling
awkward and alien
knowing no one
quite like me
out there in the
world.

and so..
the shame/blame game

continued despite
years of therapy
and meditation
praying to every single
diety that i had
ever heard of
(and some i hadn't)
still the one true thing i knew -
the temple of my familiar
was my brokeness.

then one day
so tired of feeling
less than i
made the decision
to believe in my
own innate goodness
then announced to
the world
(and even more
importantly, to myself)
that i, kit love
was worthy of love.

and i hope that those
deities that i prayed
to so fervently can
hear my offering of
gratitude; because i am
not entirely certain what
precipitated this decision
to love myself
after so many decades
of alienation.

perhaps the gods
just took pity on me,
watching me struggle
so desperately
for eons and eons

finally granting
me my only wish -
which was to belong
to the world,
even so.

lost and found

i'm mourning the loss
of my beloved puppy
lucille pearl love.
i'm mourning the loss
of sitting at the family
table singing chanukah
songs with all my relations.

i'm mourning the loss of
my innocent heart, since
she who promised to
love me forever, told
me on one very cold
christmas eve that
she was leaving me,
taking my favourite cat
polly with her.

when i asked her about
her promise of forever
she said and i quote here
'forever is a very long time.'

i'm mourning the loss
of my knee cartilage,
and the promise of
ever completing the
boston marathon
in under two hours.

i'm mourning the loss
of my ingenue status
and of seeing my name
on the cover of all the glossy
magazines.

i'm mourning the loss
of all my addictions -
humpty dumpty potato
chips no longer my
constant nighttime
companions.

i'm mourning the loss
of my very last hiding
place. i bid adieu to
cowering in the closet,
this space too small now to
house my soul.

all that is left is
this moment, this
very second, where slowly,
yet ever so tenderly,
i place my trembling
right hand on my
still beating heart,
breathing deeply in
and then breathing
deeply out.

and in this moment,
and for this moment,
this is enough.

the importance of grief

i don't remember my
childhood really,
i just have vague memories
of feeling lost, lonely and
alone.

i do remember the dearth
of tenderness that i both
needed and wanted
so badly though
i had no words
nor feelings to articulate
that need
for the language
spoken in my
family was lies
but lies did not come
easily to me as i
spoke truth as
my mother tongue,
which then exacerbated
the violence against me
ten fold.

finally after many false
starts i too became
an expert on violence but
not against others
but against, of course,
myself.

my tribe was large
so many people acting
cruelly to each other
in the guise of love.

power over was seen
as the penultimate
act of bravery, complete
dominion the first.

i tried as a child
i did; i tried so hard
to speak my truth
to their power,

but that just made me
a bigger target and
in this particular family
i was often and only
their sole target practice.

the verse that was sung
and stung worse than
one thousand bee stings
over and over without
end was this:
why are you so weird?
weird was this group's
swear word as conformity
to society's norm
was the prize
so to a person both
little and big
i was ostracized,
bullied, violated
and worse of all,
ignored ..

so i learned
to turn their violence
unto myself.

i was such a good student
producing the best results
so that no one

could hurt me
more than i would
hurt myself.

i became a model
spectre, i was
there but not really
as i had annihilated
myself into
oblivion or maybe
beyond.

then, one night a
few years ago
i was watching
a funeral on tv
for our late prime minister
brian mulroney
his children
sobbing,
i thought to myself

"i wonder what it would
feel like to love someone
that much?"
i felt jealous of their ability
to love their father so deeply.

i wished i could
experience both deep
love and deep loss
because it felt to me
that night, as if grief
might be a gateway,
a conduit to something
bigger, perhaps a portal,
a path to experiencing love.

so i who said "i always
wake up happy!"

began to question
if that was actually true
and began to feel
for the first time how
my sadness might not
be another swear word
but actually an opportunity
to fully experience my
humaneness.

and till this day though
it's still always scary
i give myself
the gift of grief
because if i can't
feel my grief then
i can't feel my love
or ecstasy or
awe at just being alive
to finally feel
the beauty of my
brokenness ~

day one

how many times have i written
those two words?
as my daughter used to say
when she was a child -
a billion trillion times.

there is something so
blindly hopeful about
fresh starts and
new beginnings,
particularly poignant
since i have indeed
begun again and
again and again and..

but it is october 11th
which happens to be
the day i chose to
incarnate once again,
and this morning whilst
walking my puppy
georgia gray, we came
across a pale pink rose
her petals perfect in
all her faded glory,
and i turned to my
beatific puppy and
said "what a perfect
day to begin anew."
and i could see in
her big brown
button eyes, that
she agreed with me,
perfectly.

splash!

something, some
centrifugal force
keeps you paddling,
your right arm
stretched out
cupping the waves
in your hand
as you blindly
reach towards
the shore ~

then the next
stroke, then
the next,
kicking your feet
now to get
some traction,
some extra movement~
one more propulsion,
one big splash.

sometimes you feel
as if you will never
make it to the
shore at all
but slowly sink
into the inky indigo
coloured water,

but then, just as
you were about
to surrender
to the sea,

the tip of your toes
touches the rippled

sand, and you
allow your body
to relax, because
against all the
incredible odds,
you've finally
reached your
beach.